**W9-BVV-043**

# SCOOBY-DOO!

# A STATES OF MATTER MYSTERY

## REVENGE FROM A WATERY GRAVE

By Megan Cooley Peterson

illustrated by Christian Cornia

CAPSTONE PRESS
a capstone imprint

Waves bubbled onto the shore as the gang hung out at the beach.

"Man, my ice pop keeps melting!" Shaggy said.

"That's no surprise on a hot day like today," Daphne said. "Ice plus heat equals liquid."

"Ragic!" Scooby said.

"It's not magic, Scooby," Velma said. "It's simple science. Everything around us is made of matter. It's either a solid, liquid, or gas. But heat or cold can often turn matter from one of those states into another."

Shaggy looked confused.

"What's the matter, Shaggy?" Daphne asked.

"The *matter* is that my solid ice pop turned to liquid before I could eat it!" Shaggy complained.

"You totally ruined these delicious hot dogs, Scoob," moaned Shaggy.

Scooby pointed toward the water. "Rhost!"

"I see a hazy cloud," Daphne said. "Is that where you saw the ghost, Scooby?"

Scooby nodded.

"Not so fast, Scooby," Velma said. "That's probably just fog, not a ghost."

"Fog happens when warm, moist air passes over a cool surface—like the ocean," Fred explained.

"Air has water vapor in it, which is the gas form of water," Velma continued. "When the air can't hold any more water, that vapor condenses into tiny water droplets and creates fog."

"So ice is water's solid form, and vapor is its gas form? Water sure does have a lot of disguises!" Shaggy said.

"Yep. Many substances can exist in more than one state of matter," explained Fred. "Just not at the same time."

"All I know is, the state of my belly is empty!" said Shaggy.

"Rine roo," agreed Scooby.

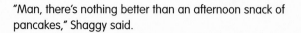

"Man, there's nothing better than an afternoon snack of pancakes," Shaggy said.

"Res!" said Scooby, digging in.

"But I wish this syrup would stay on my cakes," Shaggy said. "It's running onto the table!"

"That's because liquids, like syrup, have no shape of their own. They take on whatever shape you put them in," Daphne explained.

"Listen to this," said Velma. "Another yacht vanished from the marina last night. The sheriff and coast guard are baffled."

Daphne leaned over to read the article. "A local surfer claims the ghost of Captain Cutler stole the yacht."

Shaggy dropped his fork. "Did you say g-ghost?"

"R-rhost?" echoed Scooby.

"Maybe that strange cloud at the beach really was a ghost," Daphne said.

"Let's track down that surfer," Fred suggested.

ANOTHER YACHT
MYSTERIOUSLY VANISHES

"I saw Cutler's ghost, all right," said the surfer. "Right before the boat disappeared."

"What makes you think it's the ghost of Captain Cutler?" asked Daphne.

The surfer grabbed her board. "On a warm summer's night last year, a yacht from the marina crashed into Captain Cutler's ship. His boat sank in the graveyard of ships."

"Captain Cutler's ghost must be seeking revenge," guessed Fred.

"Is the old captain making all this spooky smoke too?" wondered Shaggy.

"That's not smoke," said Velma. "It's more fog, Shaggy."

"Zoinks!" shouted Shaggy. "It's the ghost of Captain Cutler!"

"It's not the ghost," said Velma. "It's only Scooby-Doo."

"What are you doing with that old diving suit?" Fred asked.

"I'm donating it," the surfer said. "I'm going to hit the waves.
You should visit the captain's wife. She runs the old lighthouse."

"Man, this place is spookier than a haunted house at Halloween," said Shaggy.

"Are you Mrs. Cutler?" Velma asked.

The woman stirred the pot. "I am, dearie. What can I do for you?"

"We think we saw Captain Cutler's ghost in the marina," Velma explained. "Do you know anything about that?"

"Why, yes," said Mrs. Cutler. "I used witchcraft to bring back his ghost from its watery grave."

Shaggy swallowed. "So it's true that the captain's ghost has been stealing boats?"

"I'm afraid so," Mrs. Cutler said. "Had I known his ghost would seek revenge, I would have left him under the sea."

"Wait, Scoob!" shouted Shaggy. "Don't eat that! It's the ghost!"

"It's not a ghost, Shaggy," said Fred. "It's only steam."

"Ream?" asked Scooby.

Velma nodded. "When water boils, it begins to turn into water vapor—a liquid turning into a gas because of heat."

"All matter is made of atoms, or groups of atoms called molecules," Daphne added. "As the water heats up, the molecules at the top vibrate very quickly. Some of the molecules escape as a gas. That's called evaporation."

"I think we should evaporate ourselves out of this creepy place," Shaggy muttered.

## FACT FILE

Steam is an invisible gas. The cloud above boiling water is actually the steam condensing back into a liquid, which you can see.

"The air is getting chilly," Daphne said.

"Yeah, I can't tell if I'm shivering from the cold or because Mrs. Cutler gave me the creeps," Shaggy said.

"Reeps!" Scooby agreed with a shudder.

"Our next step is to find that ghost," said Velma.

A green glow skittered across the beach. "Zoinks! Is every creepy monster in town at the beach today?" asked Shaggy.

"After that glow, Scooby-Doo!" Fred shouted.

"It's only seaweed," Daphne said. "What do you think it means?"

"According to my research, this type of seaweed glows. And it only comes from one place," Velma said.

Shaggy gulped. "I'm afraid to ask."

"The graveyard of ships!" Velma exclaimed. "That's where Captain Cutler's ship sank."

"Man, I'm so spooked my breath is trying to run away," said Shaggy.

"Your breath is a gas, just like air," Velma said. "It escapes if it's not in a container. But when the air is cold enough, it turns the water vapor in your breath into tiny liquid or even solid particles. That's what you're seeing."

"Speaking of things we can see, I'd like to see that graveyard of ships. Let's rent a boat," Fred said.

## FACT FILE

Our breath is a gas that contains water vapor. When it's cold enough outside, you can see your breath. That's because the cold air freezes the water vapor in your breath as you exhale, turning gas into tiny particles of ice.

"Here we are," said Fred. "The graveyard of ships."

"Rooky," said Scooby, shivering.

"Look!" Shaggy shouted. "It's one of the yachts from the marina!"

"And it's heading straight into that cave," said Daphne.

"But there's no one aboard," Velma said. "And the motor's not running. How is it moving?"

"It must be the ghost!" cried Shaggy.

Fred steered toward the cave. "There's only one way to find out. Let's follow that boat!"

"Something's wrong," Daphne said. "The boat vanished!"

"Zoinks! Captain Cutler's ghost must have taken it to the underworld," cried Shaggy.

"It couldn't have sailed through that rock wall," Daphne said. "Rock is a solid."

"And unlike liquids and gases, solids hold their shapes," Velma added. "That's because a solid's atoms and molecules stick tightly together."

"Come on, gang," said Fred. "Let's check out one of the sunken ships."

"This spooky ship is the perfect home for that sea-going ghost," Shaggy said.

"Rhost!" Scooby shouted as the door to the ship's cabin suddenly closed.

"I think that ghost just locked us in!" cried Daphne.

"Yep, we're trapped behind this steel door," said Fred.

"Too bad we can't melt the door like my ice pop," Shaggy said. "If it were a liquid, we could swim right through it."

"Solids usually *do* have melting points," Velma said. "Steel has a melting point of 2,500 degrees Fahrenheit, or about 1,400 degrees Celsius."

"That'd be some pretty hot steel stew!" said Shaggy.

"Very hot," agreed Velma. "At that temperature, the atoms start to release each other, so the steel becomes a liquid."

"Well, I don't think we'll be melting this door," Daphne said. "Any other ideas?"

"Ringrot?" Scooby suggested, holding up Shaggy's slingshot.

"Nice work, Scooby!" Daphne said.

"Our slingshot, like, totally saved the day," added Shaggy. "No science needed."

"Actually, you did use science," Velma said. "When you stretch a solid, the atoms pull apart. When you let go, they snap back together like a rubber band."

"Great work, gang. Let's keep exploring," said Fred.

"It's a secret stash of air tanks," said Daphne.

"And they glow, just like the seaweed," Fred added.

"Things are beginning to make sense," Velma said.
"We need to get a closer look at that ghost."

Scooby pointed at some glowing footprints on the ground.
"Rootrints!" he said.

"Follow those prints, Scoob!" Fred said.

The gang followed the footprints off the ship's deck and onto an underwater ledge in the cavern.

"The footprints vanish into that rock wall!" exclaimed Daphne.

"Something fishy is going on," Velma said.

"Rishy," Scooby agreed.

"Man, I thought you said rocks were solid," Shaggy said, backing away. "It must really be a ghost if it can walk through that!" Scooby tripped and tried to catch his fall.

"Look!" Fred shouted. "Shaggy found a secret passage!"

"And it leads directly into another cavern filled with stolen yachts from the marina," said Velma.

"Mystery solved," said Shaggy. "Time to go home."

"Not so fast," Fred said. "We've still got to catch the ghost!"

"I was afraid you'd say that," muttered Shaggy.

"What's your plan, Fred?" asked Daphne.

Fred turned on an ice-making machine. "This machine freezes water and turns it into ice," he explained. "We'll coat the ramp with ice. When the ghost shows up, he'll slip into our net."

"Changing a liquid into a solid," said Velma.
"Science wins again!"

"We better hurry," said Shaggy. "Who knows when that creepy ghost will show its face again!"

"Right row!" shouted Scooby.

"Zoinks! The ghost, like, slipped right into our trap," said Shaggy.

"Let's find out who this ghost really is," said Fred. He pulled off the ghost's diving helmet.

"It's Captain Cutler!" exclaimed Shaggy.

"Rit ris?" asked Scooby.

"It's him all right. We saw his picture at the lighthouse," explained Velma.

"Captain Cutler and his wife cooked up this whole ghost story," explained Daphne. "They stole those yachts from the marina."

"And planned to sell them for a hefty profit," Fred added.

"Captain Cutler used this portable steam machine to look like a ghost," Velma said.

"And we would have gotten away with it if it weren't for you meddling kids!" said Mrs. Cutler.

"Solid work, team!" Fred said.

"Pass me a marshmallow, will you Scoob?" asked Shaggy. "This time, I *want* my solid to melt! Yum!"

# GLOSSARY

**atom** (AT-uhm)—the smallest particle of an element

**condense** (kuhn-DENS)—to change from gas to liquid; water vapor condenses into liquid water

**evaporation** (i-vap-uh-RAY-shun)—the act of turning from a liquid to a gas

**gas** (GASS)—something that is not solid or liquid and does not have a definite shape

**liquid** (LIK-wid)—matter that is wet and can be poured, such as water

**matter** (MAT-uhr)—anything that has weight and takes up space

**molecule** (MOL-uh-kyool)—the atoms making up the smallest unit of a substance; $H_2O$ is a molecule of water

**solid** (SOL-id)—a substance that holds its shape

**steam** (STEEM)—the vapor that water turns into when it boils

**water vapor** (WAH-tuhr VAY-puhr)—water in gas form; water vapor is one of many invisible gases in air

# SCIENCE AND ENGINEERING PRACTICES

1. Asking questions (for science) and defining problems (for engineering)

2. Developing and using models

3. Planning and carrying out investigations

4. Analyzing and interpreting data

5. Using mathematics and computational thinking

6. Constructing explanations (for science) and designing solutions (for engineering)

7. Engaging in argument from evidence

8. Obtaining, evaluating, and communicating information

Next Generation Science Standards

# READ MORE

**Larson, Karen.** *Changing Matter.* Huntington Beach, Calif.: Teacher Created Materials, 2015.

**Slade, Suzanne.** *Splat! Wile E. Coyote Experiments with States of Matter.* Wile E. Coyote, Physical Science Genius. North Mankato, Minn.: Capstone Press, 2014.

**Slingerland, Janet.** *Werewolves and States of Matter.* Monster Science. Mankato, Minn.: Capstone Press, 2012.

# INTERNET SITES

FactHound offers a safe, fun way to find Internet sites related to this book. All of the sites on FactHound have been researched by our staff.

Here's all you do:

Visit *www.facthound.com*

Type in this code: 9781515725923

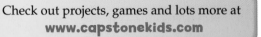

Check out projects, games and lots more at **www.capstonekids.com**

Super-cool stuff!

# INDEX

Thanks to our adviser for his expertise, research, and advice:
Paul Ohmann, PhD, Associate Professor of Physics
University of St. Thomas, St. Paul, Minnesota

Published in 2016 by Capstone Press, A Capstone Imprint
1710 Roe Crest Drive, North Mankato, Minnesota 56003
www.mycapstone.com

**Library of Congress Cataloging-in-Publication Data**
Names: Peterson, Megan Cooley, author.
Title: Scooby-Doo! a states of matter mystery : revenge from a watery grave /
by Megan Cooley Peterson.
Other titles: States of matter mystery
Description: North Mankato, Minnesota : Capstone Press, a Capstone imprint,
[2016] | 2016 | Series: Scooby-Doo!. Scooby-Doo solves it with S.T.E.M. |
Includes bibliographical references and index. |
Audience: ages 9-12. | Audience: grades 4 to 6.
Identifiers: LCCN 2015043267 | ISBN 9781515725923 (library binding) | ISBN 9781515726531 (ebook PDF) |
Subjects: LCSH: Matter—Properties—Juvenile literature. |
Matter—Constitution—Juvenile literature. | Scooby-Doo (Fictitious character)—Juvenile literature.
Classification: LCC QC173.36 .P48 2017 | DDC 530.4—dc23
LC record available at http://lccn.loc.gov/2015043267

**Editorial Credits**
Editor: Kristen Mohn
Designer: Ashlee Suker
Creative Director: Nathan Gassman
Production Specialist: Gene Bentdahl
The illustrations in this book were created digitally.

Printed in the United States of America.
032016        009681F16

# OTHER TITLES IN THIS SET: